Do you have a passion for wood pallets? Then get ready to indulge yourself with crafty projects that transform wood pieces into unique home accessories and gifts. Make a few simple cuts, add some decorative trims or finishes, and enjoy the compliments on your creations!

LEISURE ARTS, INC. • Maumelle, Arkansas

Fence-Style Frame

Instructions on page 14.

Photo Collage

Instructions on page 16.

Frame

Instructions on page 20.

Flower Panels

Instructions on page 21.

A B C

Instructions on page 22.

Coat Rack

Instructions on page 23.

Tray

Instructions on page 24.

Clock

Instructions on page 26.

Memories

Instructions on page 27.

Hope

Instructions on page 28.

Fence-Style Frame

Shown on pages 2-3.

Finished Size: determined by the size of your artwork (our frame is approximately 40" x 38")

SHOPPING LIST

- ☐ shipping pallet
- ☐ pre-painted artist stretched canvas (we used a 38" x 30" piece of artwork)
- ☐ large towel or blanket (to cover work surface)
- ☐ tools and supplies (refer to page 30 and instructions, below)

To make the Frame:

For ease of insertion, follow Making a Pilot Hole, page 31, when using screws to join wood pieces or attach items to wood.

1. Refer to the Basic Instructions, pages 30-31, to take apart the pallet and prepare the boards.

2. From the prepared pallet boards, cut 5 vertical boards 6" - 12" longer than height of your artwork (look for boards with character, such as knots or nail holes and unique grain patterns). For the braces, cut 2 horizontal boards 4" longer than width of your artwork (these boards will need to be sturdy, without any splits in the wood or knot holes).

Designed by Max Farrell.

3. Place your canvas face down on the towel or blanket. Center one brace on the wood frame at the top of the canvas. Being careful not to go all the way through to the front of the canvas, drill pilot holes through the brace and into the canvas frame about 2" from either top corner of the canvas; insert screws in the holes. **Note:** Check your screw length before inserting. It should be long enough to go through the brace and into the canvas frame but short enough to not go through to the canvas front. Repeat at the bottom of the canvas for the remaining brace ***(Fig. 1)***.

4. Spacing as desired, arrange the vertical boards across the width of the canvas. When satisfied with placement drill pilot holes through the boards and into the canvas frame at the top and bottom of the canvas; attach the boards to the frame with screws ***(Fig. 2)***.

5. Still working from the back, attach a sawtooth hanger to the first and last vertical boards, just below the top edge of the canvas.

Fig. 1

Fig. 2

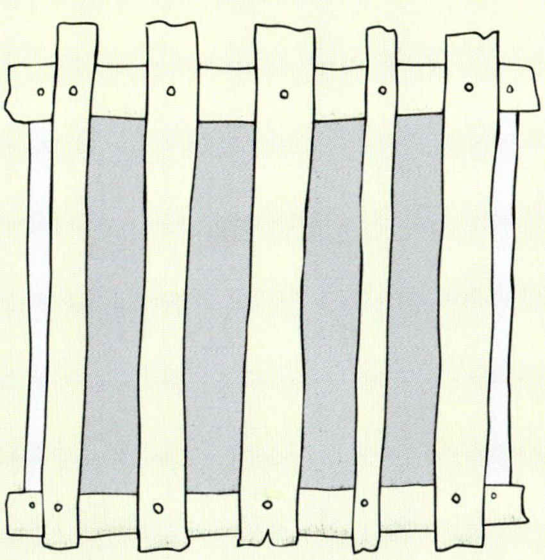

Photo Collage

Shown on page 4.

Finished Size: approximately 70" x 60"

This pallet wood frame is perfect for showing off your favorite family photos. We chose to print our two largest photos onto artist stretched canvas. The remaining photos are printed on regular photo paper and mounted on burlap covered stretched canvases. You may choose to use a variety of different size photos as we did (ranging from 5" x 7" to 12" x 16"), use four large photos, or even two large and six small pictures. There are lots of possibilities so it's time to get creative ! Turn to page 19 for some ideas!

SHOPPING LIST

- ☐ 2 shipping pallets or 1 pallet and 5 additional weathered wood pieces
- ☐ photo(s) printed on artist stretched canvas then mounted on stretcher strips (we used a 12" x 16" photo and a 9" x 12" photo) **Note:** most full service camera and photo processing shops offer this service
- ☐ photo(s) printed on photo paper (we used 2 8" x 10" and 3 5" x 7" photos)
- ☐ burlap covered stretched canvases (we used 2 8" x 10" and 3 5" x 7" canvases) **OR** artist stretched canvases to cover in the same sizes, burlap fabric, staple gun and staples
- ☐ roofing shingle*
- ☐ heavy object picture hanging kit
- ☐ tools and supplies (refer to pages 30-31 and instructions, right)

* We used a piece of a shingle for the photo holder corner triangles. You could also use coarse grit sandpaper or cork for a similar look. Decorative vintage metal corners are another option.

To make the Frame:

For ease of insertion, follow Making a Pilot Hole, page 31, when using screws to join wood pieces or attach items to wood.

1. Refer to the Basic Instructions, pages 30-31, to take apart the pallets and prepare the boards.

2. For the frame, cut 2 top/bottom boards each 70" long. Cut 2 side boards each 60" long and 1 center board 50" long.

3. For the panels, cut 8 Panel 1 boards each 44" long. Cut 8 Panel 2 boards each 22" long.

4. Working from the wrong side, arrange the frame boards on large flat surface, as shown in **Fig. 1**. **Note:** Your spacing may differ slightly based on the width of your boards.

5. Drill 2 pilot holes at each intersection of the boards and insert screws ***(Fig. 2)***.

Tips

For a secure hold when attaching a board to a board, be sure your screws are long enough to go completely through the top board and 1/2 - 3/4 of the way through the second board.

Take the shine off nail and screw heads with a little dab of acrylic paint. Choose black or dark brown to make new hardware appear vintage.

Designed by Max Farrell.

Fig. 1

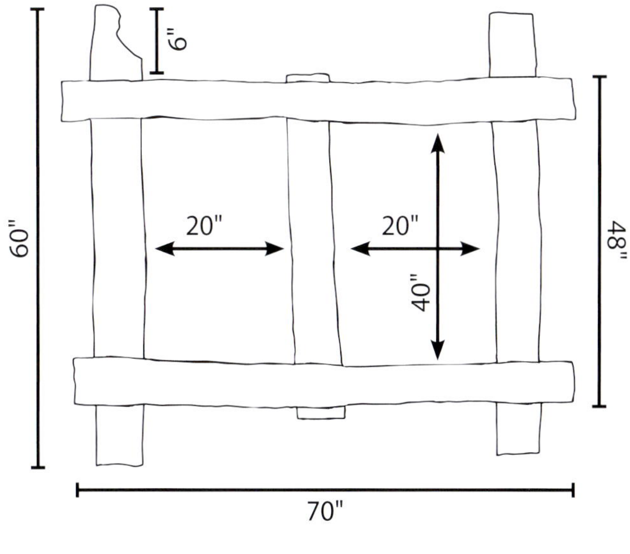

Fig. 2

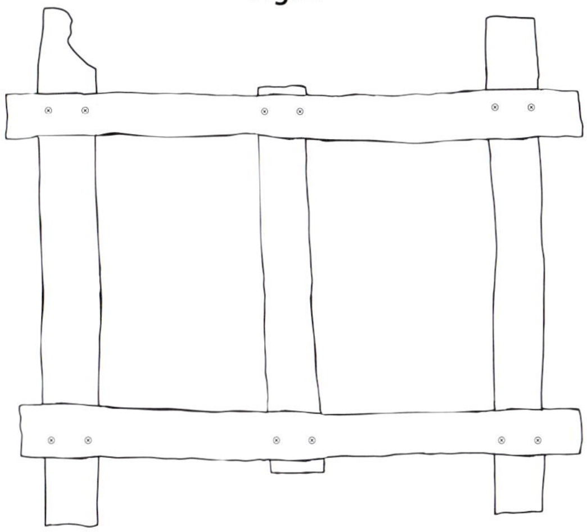

Fig. 3

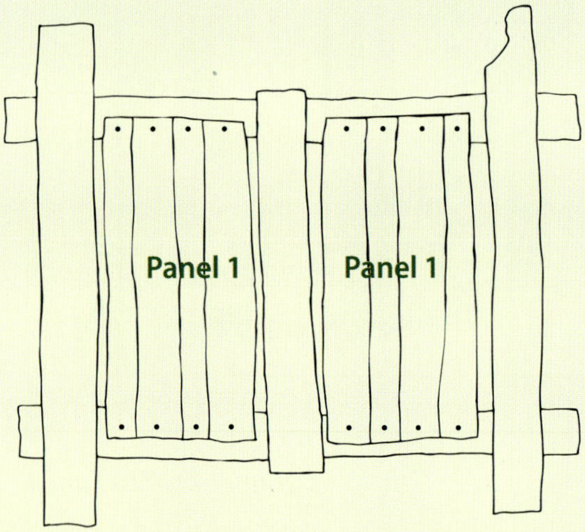

Fig. 4

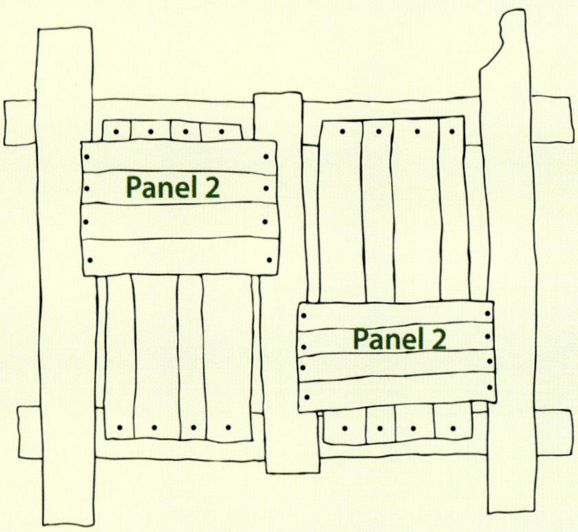

Fig. 5

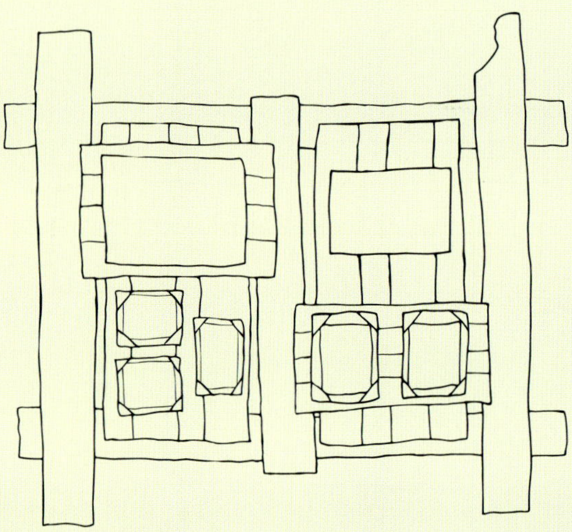

6. Working from the right side, use 1 nail in the top and bottom of each Panel 1 board to secure it to the frame *(Fig. 3)*.

7. Working from the right side, use 1 nail in each end of each Panel 2 board to secure it to the frame *(Fig.4)*.

8. Follow the manufacturer's instructions to attach the picture hanging kit to the back of the frame.

9. If using burlap-covered canvases, skip to Step 10. To cover artist stretched canvases with burlap see Covering A Stretched Canvas, below.

10. For photo corners, cut 4 squares 2" x 2" from the shingle; cut each square in half diagonally. Place one photo corner $^1/_2$" from one corner of a burlap canvas. Using a screw long enough to go through the photo corner, and into the canvas frame, secure the photo corner. Repeat for each photo corner.

11. To hang the photos, drive small nails into the Panels and hang the canvases on the nails. This makes it easy to switch out the canvases when you have new photos *(Fig. 5)*.

Covering A Stretched Canvas

1. Measure the width of the canvas including the sides and add 1". Repeat to measure the height of the canvas. Cut a rectangle of burlap the determined measurements. Place the canvas face down in the center of the burlap.

2. Fold one side of the burlap up and around to the back of the canvas. Staple the burlap in place along the length of the wood frame. Pulling the fabric taut, repeat along the opposite side.

3. Repeat Step 2 on the two remaining sides. For the corners, trim the excess fabric as needed then neatly fold and staple the fabric to the wood frame.

Get Creative!

Want your photo collage to be a little different? Check out these suggestions.

Make a copy or copies of the You Design Diagram, below, for sketching alternate arrangements for your photos and items.

Make a Memory Collage by including some framed maps, ticket stubs, postcards, and other memorabilia.

Use photo transfer medium to mount a photograph on a wood plaque (see page 27, Steps 2-6).

You may even want to include a shadow box frame with items you have collected such as sea shells or pressed flowers.

You Design Diagram

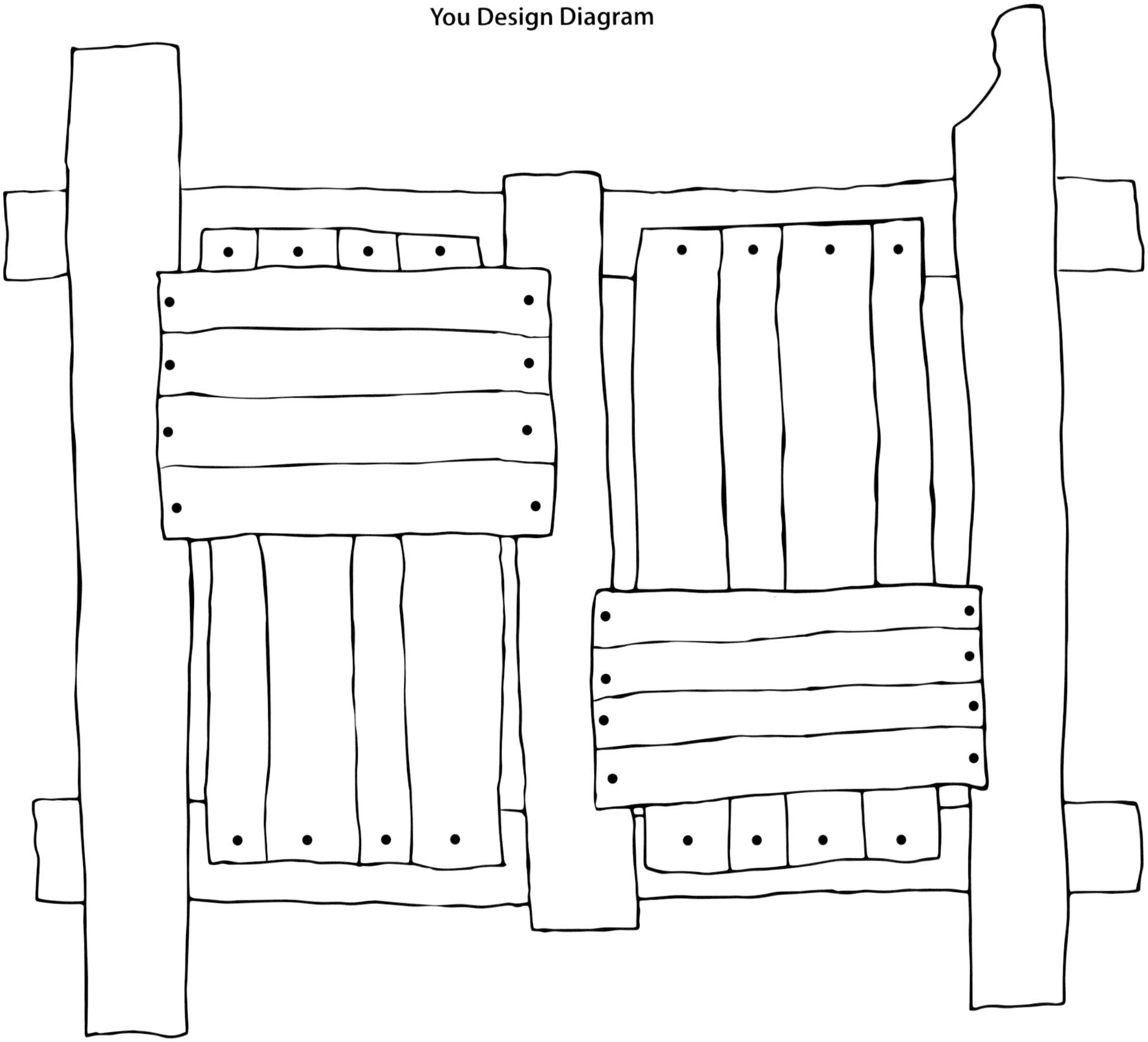

Leisure Arts, Inc. grants the owner of this book permission to photocopy the diagram on page 19 for personal use only.

FRAME

Shown on page 5.

Finished Size: approximately 16" x 14"

Designed by Max Farrell.

SHOPPING LIST

- ☐ 4 approximately 3 1/2" x 16" shipping pallet boards
- ☐ 9 1/2" x 11 1/2" x 1/4" rectangle of bead board
- ☐ vintage door lock plate (approximately 8" high)
- ☐ 8" x 10" photograph
- ☐ black acrylic paint (matte)
- ☐ 4" x 6" piece of roofing shingle*
- ☐ clear acrylic sealer (matte)
- ☐ bar clamp (optional)
- ☐ tools and supplies (refer to page 30 and instructions, right)

* We used a piece of a shingle for the photo holder corner triangles. You could also use coarse grit sandpaper or cork for a similar look. Decorative vintage metal corners are another option.

To make the Frame:

For ease of insertion, follow Making a Pilot Hole, page 31, when using screws to join wood pieces or attach items to wood.

1. Refer to the Basic Instructions, pages 30-31 to prepare the boards.
2. With cut ends aligned, glue the boards together along the long edges. **Tip:** Using a bar clamp will hold the boards tightly together while the glue dries.
3. For the photo backer, paint the bead board rectangle black. When completely dry, sand with fine grit sandpaper to remove some paint and give the wood a distressed look. Apply a coat of clear acrylic sealer; allow to dry.
4. Arrange the lock plate and photo backer on the pallet wood rectangle. When satisfied with the arrangement, glue the photo backer in place. Use screws to attach the lock plate. Paint the screw heads black.
5. For the photo corners, cut 2 squares 2" x 2" from the shingle piece; cut each square in half diagonally. Place one photo corner 1/2" from one corner of the photo backer. Using a screw long enough to go through the photo corner, photo backer and into the pallet wood, secure the photo corner. Repeat for each photo corner. Paint the screw heads black. Insert the photograph under the photo corners.

Tip

To hang, center and attach a sawtooth hanger close to the top edge on the back of the panel.

FLOWER PANELS

Shown on page 6.

Finished Size: 10" x 10" each, not including flowers

Designed by Megan Russell.

SHOPPING LIST

- ☐ 2 10" x 10" slatted wood panels with jute hangers
- ☐ 2 6" high glass milk jars
- ☐ chalk paint (white)
- ☐ 1" wide flat paintbrush
- ☐ green jute twine
- ☐ clear acrylic sealer (matte)
- ☐ Locktite® Go2™ Glue multipurpose adhesive
- ☐ 2 small bunches of assorted real or artificial flowers
- ☐ tools and supplies (refer to page 30 and instructions, right)

To make one Flower Panel:

1. Refer to the Basic Instructions, pages 30-31, to prepare a panel.
2. Paint a bottle white and allow to dry.
3. To dry brush the panel, use the flat brush and dip the bristle tips in the paint, wipe off excess on a paper towel. Working horizontally, lightly brush the paint across the slats. **Note:** Always wipe the excess paint off on a paper towel before brushing on the panel.
4. With the bottom of the bottle even with the bottom edge of the panel, center the bottle horizontally on the panel. Use a pencil to mark a drill hole on either side of the bottle neck; remove the bottle. Drill a small (about 1/8") hole at each mark. Glue the bottle to the center of the panel between the drill holes.
5. Cut a 36" length of twine. Working from back to front, thread the twine ends through the drilled holes. Wrap the twine twice around the bottle neck and tie a bow at the center front; trim the twine ends to about 2". Arrange the flowers in the bottle.

ABC

Shown on page 7.

One of the cool things about this project is the ability to customize. Our letters are 12" high on an 18" x18" panel made from a pallet, but you could easily use larger or smaller letters. The width is the determined by the number and width of the pallet boards. Once you determine the width, just cut your pallet boards that length to make the panel square. If you are using tall skinny letters, cut the pallet boards longer.

SHOPPING LIST

- ☐ shipping pallet with 3 1/2" - 4" wide boards
- ☐ 6 approximately 2" x 16" x 1/2" boards for the cross braces
- ☐ acrylic paint (blue, red, and yellow)
- ☐ 12" high bronze polystone letters A, B, C
- ☐ 3 2" long sawtooth hangers
- ☐ 1" wide flat paintbrush
- ☐ small foam plates
- ☐ E6000® Industrial Strength Adhesive
- ☐ tools and supplies (refer to page 30 and instructions, right)

To make the ABC panels:

1. Refer to the Basic Instructions, pages 30-31, to take apart the pallets and prepare the boards. Cut 14-16 18" lengths from the pallet boards.

2. Arrange 4-5 pallet boards side by side until they measure about 18" wide. With the cut ends aligned, place the boards wrong side up on your work surface. Apply wood glue to the wrong side of one cross brace. Keeping the boards close together, position a cross brace about 2" below the top edge of the boards; press down firmly. Repeat to add a second cross brace about 2" above the bottom edge of the boards.

3. Still working from the wrong side and using screws that are long enough to go through the cross brace and into the boards, but not so long that they go through the boards, secure the cross braces to the boards with 4 evenly spaced screws.

4. Repeat Steps 2 and 3 to make 2 more panels. Center and attach a sawtooth hanger close to the top edge on the back of each panel.

Designed by Max Farrell.

5. To make the color washes, pour about a 2" circle of blue, red, and yellow paint onto separate foam plates; add about a teaspoon of water to each color and mix well. Test each color on the back of a panel. If a color is too opaque, add more water. If a color is too translucent, add more paint. When satisfied with the look, use the flat brush to paint each panel a different color; allow to dry.

6. Center and adhere one letter to each panel.

Initial It Your Way!

We used bronze polystone letters for our panels, but with letters available in so many fonts and materials, some other options include wood, papier-mâché, metal, and chipboard. For a custom look, you can paint, stain, or leave your letters natural!

COAT RACK

Designed by Max Farrell.

Shown on pages 8-9.

What do you make when you run across a sturdy pallet board with natural weathering, unusual knot holes and a distinctive grain? With that much character your board is crying out to be the star of a project, so you turn it into a coat rack!

Start with a pressure washing, sanding with a medium then fine grit sandpaper, and wiping down with a soft cloth. You can leave your board natural or add light coat of stain.

Working from the back, install a sawtooth hanger close to each end and in the middle of the board. On the front, use a pencil to mark the placement for 4 evenly spaced coat hooks. Make a Pilot Hole, page 31, at each mark and use wood screws to attach the coat hooks.

Tip

Always check the length of your wood screws before inserting to be sure they are not longer than the depth of your wood plus any item (such as a coat hook) you may be attaching.

TRAY

Shown on page 10.

This tray looks as though the boards were pulled right off side of an old barn, when they actually came in a bundle from a craft store! Precut into handy lengths and bundled together, these wood pieces make it super easy to craft this personalized tray!

Finished Size: approximately $8^{5}/_{8}$" x 14" x $^{5}/_{8}$"

SHOPPING LIST

- ☐ 8 $1^{5}/_{8}$" x 14" x $^{5}/_{8}$" natural barn wood boards
- ☐ 2 approximately $5^{1}/_{2}$" long black metal drawer pulls
- ☐ acrylic paint (cream)
- ☐ 5" high letter stencil
- ☐ small stencil brush
- ☐ painter's tape
- ☐ foam plate
- ☐ Locktite® Go2™ Glue multipurpose adhesive
- ☐ tools and supplies (refer to page 30 and instructions, right)

To make the Tray:

For ease of insertion, follow Making a Pilot Hole, page 31, when using screws to join wood pieces or attach items to wood.

1. Refer to the Basic Instructions, pages 30-31, to prepare the boards.

2. With the short ends aligned, place 6 boards, right side up, close together on your work surface; measure the width. From the remaining 2 boards cut 2 crossbars this measurement. Apply wood glue to the wrong side of one crossbar. Keeping the boards close together, position the crossbar on one end of the boards even with the board ends; press down firmly. Repeat to add a second crossbar to the other end of the boards ***(Fig. 1)***.

Designed by Kelly Reider.

3. Working from the wrong side and using screws that are long enough to go through the boards and into, but not through, the crossbars, secure the crossbars to the tray with 6 evenly spaced screws ***(Fig. 2)***.

4. Center the stencil on the tray and secure with painter's tape. Pour a small amount paint onto a foam plate; add a few drops of water and mix well.

5. Test the color on a scrap from the crossbar. If the color is too opaque, add more water. If the color is too translucent, add more paint. When satisfied with the look, fill in the stencil with an up and down pouncing motion; allow to dry. For a distressed look, lightly sand the letter with fine-grit sand paper.

6. Center and adhere one handle to each cross bar.

Fig. 1

Fig. 2

Clock

Shown on page 11.

For a super quick project for yourself or to use as a gift, check out this pallet-style clock!

Designed by Kelly Reider.

Start with an unfinished $12\frac{1}{2}$" diameter round slatted wood panel. After sanding with a medium and then a fine grit sandpaper, wipe the panel with a soft cloth. Apply a coat of stain in your favorite wood-tone shade; wipe away the excess and allow to dry. If a darker shade is desired, apply a second coat of stain.

Use painter's tape to secure $1\frac{1}{2}$" high number stencils at the 12, 3, 6, and 9 o'clock positions on the panel front. Use a small stencil brush and an up and down pouncing motion to fill in the stencils with creamy-white acrylic paint. Apply a coat of matte clear acrylic sealer.

Follow the manufacturer's instructions to install a clock works movement kit between the slats of the panel. So easy– no drilling needed! Attach a sawtooth hanger to the back.

Your clock is ready to use or gift!

MEMORIES

Shown on page 12.

A reminder of a special memory will always be in view when you create a wall hanging from a favorite photo. Using photo transfer medium and a rope trimmed slatted panel makes this project oh-so-easy.

Designed by Megan Russell.

SHOPPING LIST

- ☐ 12" x 11" slatted wood panel with rope trim and hanger
- ☐ laser printed copy of a photograph (ink jet printed photo will not work)
- ☐ Mod Podge® Photo Transfer Medium
- ☐ 3" high wood word MEMORIES
- ☐ 1" wide sponge brush
- ☐ fine to medium grit sandpaper
- ☐ soft cloth
- ☐ sponge
- ☐ clear acrylic sealer (matte)
- ☐ brayer or rolling pin (optional)

To make the Memories panel:

1. Sand the panel to smooth any rough areas; wipe with a soft cloth to remove residue.

2. Using a laser printer/copier, make a copy of your photograph *in reverse* (mirror image). This is especially important if your image has words or letters. They will be backwards on the finished project if not printed in reverse. Trim the photo to the desired size, removing any white borders in the process.

3. Use the sponge brush to apply a thick coat of transfer medium to the face of the photo.

4. Place the photo face down on the panel. Working from the center out to press out any air bubbles, gently smooth the photo onto the panel. ***Tip:*** Using a brayer or rolling pin to smooth helps to insure a good bond. To dry and cure the transfer medium, allow the panel to sit undisturbed for *at least 24 hours*.

5. Dampen the cloth and the sponge. Cover the image with a damp cloth and allow to sit for 2 minutes; remove the cloth. Use the damp sponge to gently rub away the paper backing. **Note:** For a more distressed look, you may choose to sand away some of the edges of the photo or even "fade out" parts of the photo itself.

6. Allow the image and wood to dry completely.

7. Glue the word to the lower right corner of the panel. Apply a coat of acrylic sealer to the panel.

HOPE

Shown on page 13.

Soothing colors, an inspiring message, and a string art anchor come together to serve as a daily reminder that there is always hope. The random stringing on the anchor perfectly compliments the rustic look of the wood. We traced around die cut letters to spell out our word, but you could use a stencil if desired.

Designed by Kelly Reider.

SHOPPING LIST

- ☐ 15¾" x 13¾" slatted wood panel
- ☐ acrylic paint (blue, brown, cream, green, and purple)
- ☐ 18-gauge ⅝" long nails (129)
- ☐ #12 white pearl cotton
- ☐ 3" high die-cut letters to spell HOPE
- ☐ 1" wide flat paintbrush
- ☐ small round paintbrush
- ☐ hammer
- ☐ needle-nose pliers
- ☐ fine to medium grit sandpaper
- ☐ soft cloth
- ☐ craft glue
- ☐ small foam plates
- ☐ removable tape

To make the Hope panel:

Thoroughly clean brush between paint colors.

1. Sand the panel to smooth any rough areas; wipe with the soft cloth to remove residue.

2. To make the color washes, pour about a 2" circle of blue, brown, green, and purple paint onto separate foam plates; add about a teaspoon of water to each color and mix well. Test each color on the back of the panel. If a color is too opaque, add more water. If a color is too translucent, add more paint. When satisfied with the look, use the flat brush to apply each color to the panel front; allow to dry.

3. Position the die-cut letters in the top left corner of the panel; lightly draw around each letter with a sharp pencil. Use the small brush and cream paint to fill in the letters.

4. Make a photocopy of the anchor pattern. Position the pattern on the panel and secure with tape. Using the pliers to hold the nails steady, hammer in one nail at each dot on the pattern. Remove the pattern.

5. To string the anchor, tie the pearl cotton end to any nail near the top of the anchor. Working toward the bottom, wrap the nails randomly until the anchor shape is densely covered; tie off. Put a drop of glue on both the beginning and ending knots, allow to dry and trim the tails.

Photocopy the anchor pattern at 121%.

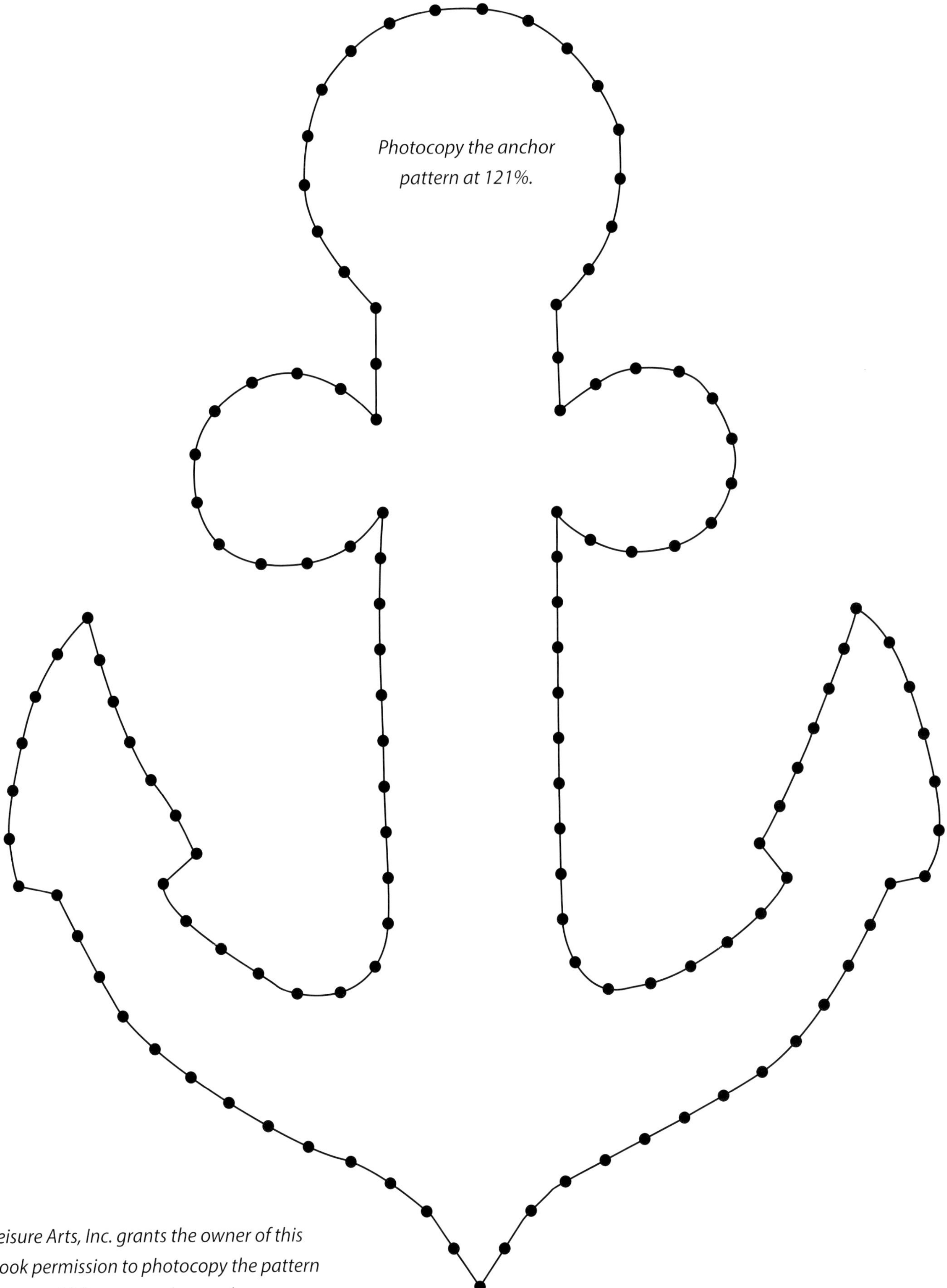

Leisure Arts, Inc. grants the owner of this book permission to photocopy the pattern on page 29 for personal use only.

BASIC INSTRUCTIONS

Some projects in this book were made by recycling used wood shipping pallets while some use unfinished pallet-style wood pieces purchased from a craft store. Some projects may be easier and faster to make using power tools such as drills, screwdrivers, saws, and sanders, but all can be completed with hand tools if preferred. ***Note:*** *A prior working knowledge of the operation and safe use of tools (power or hand) is required. This book* ***does not*** *give instruction for the use of any tools listed.*

Tools and Supplies

If you are taking apart a pallet to use the wood to construct a project, you may need several of the tools listed, but if you are using a ready-made pallet style wood panel, you may only need a few of the supplies. Be sure to read your project instructions for additional supplies specific to that project.

- ☐ hammer
- ☐ power sander and assorted sandpapers (60-150 grit) or sanding block and assorted sandpapers (60-150 grit)
- ☐ power saw or hand saw
- ☐ power drill
- ☐ power screwdriver and assorted bits or hand screwdrivers (straight and Phillips)
- ☐ pressure washer or bucket of water and a stiff natural bristle brush
- ☐ air compressor or whisk broom and soft cloths
- ☐ finishing nails (assorted sizes)
- ☐ flathead wood screws (assorted sizes)
- ☐ sawtooth hangers (assorted sizes)
- ☐ wood glue
- ☐ paper towels

Preparing a Shipping Pallet

1. Disassemble the pallet. Carefully remove all the nails. Sort the boards by size. Determine which boards are the best fit for your project. **Tip:** Pay attention to where you will be placing each board in your project. You may want to use boards with unique features such knot holes or interesting grain patterns in areas that will be seen, saving the plain ones for braces or in areas that will be covered.

2. Using a hand or power saw, cut the sizes and number of pieces called for in your project instructions.

3. Using light pressure from a pressure washer or a bucket of water and a stiff brush, clean the wood pieces to remove any dirt and bring out the character of the wood. Allow the wood to dry completely.

4. Using medium-grit sandpaper and a sanding block or a power sander, smooth any rough areas on the wood pieces. Follow with a light sanding with fine-grit sandpaper, if needed. Use compressed air, a whisk broom, or a damp cloth to remove sawdust residue. If using a damp cloth, allow the wood to dry completely.

Preparing Pallet-style Wood Pieces

1. If needed, use a hand or power saw to cut the wood piece or pieces to the size and number called for in your project instructions.

2. Using medium-grit sandpaper and a sanding block or a power sander, smooth any rough areas on the wood pieces. Follow with a light sanding with fine-grit sandpaper, if needed. Use compressed air, a whisk broom, or a damp cloth to remove sawdust residue. If using a damp cloth, allow the wood to dry completely.

Staining and Finishing the Wood:

1. Unless otherwise noted in the project instructions, all pallet wood was left its natural color. If you desired to add a stain or paint, it should be applied after the wood is prepared but before assembling the project. Allow to dry thoroughly before assembly.

2. To protect the wood, clear acrylic sealer spray or brush on can be applied once the stain is dry. Choose a matte finish to maintain the natural look of the wood. Choose a satin or gloss sealer to add shine.

Making a Pilot Hole

A pilot hole is a small hole drilled into the wood before driving in a screw. It makes it easier to insert screws into wood, keeps the wood from splitting and helps keep the screw straight as it goes into the wood. You can use this technique anytime your project instructions call for screws to be inserted.

1. Mark the location of the hole with a pencil.

2. Make an indention at the mark with a nail by striking the nail with a hammer; remove the nail. The indention will keep the bit from slipping as you drill.

3. Select a drill bit slightly smaller than the diameter of your screw. Insert the bit into the drill.

4. Holding the drill perpendicular to the wood, place the tip of the bit in the indention and drill a hole. The hole should equal the screw's length. Back the drill out.

5. Insert the screw using a hand or power screwdriver.

We have made every effort to ensure that these instructions are accurate and complete. We cannot, however, be responsible for human error, typographical mistakes, or variations in individual work.

Production Team: Technical Writer – Jean Lewis; Technical Associate – Mary Sullivan Hutcheson; Editorial Writer – Susan Frantz Wiles; Senior Graphic Artist – Lora Puls; Graphic Artist – Kellie McAnulty; Photostylist – Lori Wenger; Photographer – Jason Masters